WILD WHEELS!

Hottest Race Cars

By Erin Egan

Enslow Publishers, Inc.
40 Industrial Road
Box 398
Berkeley Heights, NJ 07922
USA
http://www.enslow.com

Library of Congress Cataloging-in-Publication Data

Egan, Erin.
  Hottest race cars / by Erin Egan.
     p. cm.
  Summary: "Read about open-wheel race cars, the drivers, and the races they compete
in, such as Formula One, the Indy Racing League, and the Champ series"—Provided by
publisher.
  Includes bibliographical references and index.
  ISBN-13: 978-0-7660-2871-5
  ISBN-10: 0-7660-2871-2
  1. Automobile racing—Juvenile literature. 2. Automobiles,
Racing—Juvenile literature. I. Title.
  GV1029.13.E43 2008
  796.72—dc22

                              2007007427

Printed in the United States of America

10 9 8 7 6 5 4 3 2

To Our Readers:
We have done our best to make sure that all Internet Addresses in this book were
active and appropriate when we went to press. However, the author and publisher have
no control over and assume no liability for the material available on those Internet sites
or on other Web sites they may link to. Any comments or suggestions can be sent by
e-mail to comments@enslow.com or to the address on the back cover.

Cover Photo: Tom Strattman /AP **Back Cover:** Associated Press/AP
Interior Photos: Alamy/Coaster, p. 18; Alamy/CrashPA, p. 27; Alamy/Mark Scheuem,
p. 24; AP/Jacques Boissinot, pp. 3, 30; AP/Fernando Bustamonte, p. 16; AP/Michael
Conroy, pp. 21, 38; AP/Darron Cummings, pp. 3, 7, 36–37; AP/Mark Duncan, p. 13;
AP/Tim Johnson, pp. 3, 20–21; AP/Dario Lopez-Mills, p. 12; AP/AJ Mast, pp. 3, 16;
AP/George Nikitin, p. 42; AP/John Raoux, p. 26; AP/Seth Rossman, p. 39; AP/Tom
Strattman, p. 35; AP/Mark J. Terrill, p. 9; Associated Press/AP, pp. 1, 10, 11, 22, 34, 44;
Todd Corzette, p. 35; Getty Images/Jeff Haynes, p. 22; Getty Images/Stan Honda, p. 39;
Getty Images/Darrell Ingham, p. 39; Getty Images/Robert Laberge, p. 28; Getty
Images/Gavin Lawrence, pp. 15, 22, 41; Getty Images/Mark Ralston, pp. 8–9; Getty
Images/Clive Rose, pp. 19, 32–33; IndyCar/Bill Watson, pp. 3, 4–5.

Contents

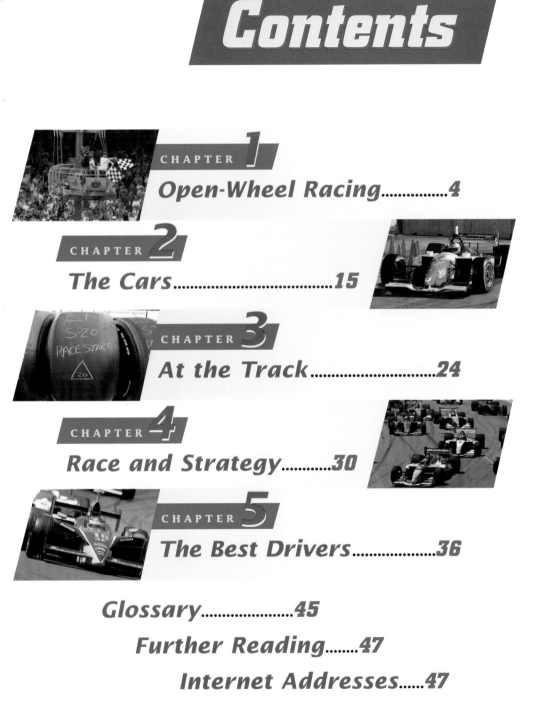

CHAPTER 1

Open-Wheel Racing

It is May 28, 2006, at the Indianapolis Motor Speedway, the largest sports arena in America. More than 300,000 people roar with excitement as sleek, colorful cars speed around the track during the Indy 500. The powerful race cars hug the ground as they

The Number 6 car driven by Sam Hornish, Jr., flies over the finish line a fraction of a second before Marco Andretti's Number 26 car. It was a dramatic finish to the 2006 Indianapolis 500.

whip around the steeply-banked corners. Their engines fill the air with an ear-rattling buzz that sounds like a huge swarm of killer bees. The cars are a blur as they travel at more than 200 miles per hour (mph). Even at those high speeds, the cars are inches apart as they head around the final turn, with the finish line dead ahead. At the last moment, one car jumps ahead and everyone is on their feet as the checkered flag is waved—Sam Hornish, Jr., has won the world's most famous car race!

It was not any ordinary victory. Hornish finished ahead of Marco Andretti by less than one-tenth of a second. It was the second-closest finish in the nearly hundred-year history of the Indy 500.

Open Wheels

The lean, mean race cars in the Indy 500 are known as open-wheel racers. They are called "open wheel" because there are no fenders covering the tires as on regular passenger cars. They are lightweight and aerodynamic (designed to cut cleanly through the air), and have extremely powerful engines. They average speeds from 187 to 220 mph. Open-wheel vehicles are raced in Formula One, Indy Racing League, and Champ Series races.

The cars hold a single driver in an open cockpit. Formula One, Indy, and Champ cars also have their engines in the back. By comparison, the cars of NASCAR have their engines in the front, and their drivers are enclosed inside the car.

Formula One

The "formula" in Formula One is the set of rules all of its drivers and cars must follow. Formula One is extremely popular around the world, especially in Europe. Its drivers come from all over the globe—Europe, North and South America, and Asia. They are as famous as rock stars, and hundreds of thousands of die-hard fans pack the tracks on race weekends worldwide. That is nearly double the number

Wheels are not the only things exposed on an open-wheel race car. The driver also sits in an open cockpit. This driver is Buddy Rice, racing in the Indianapolis 500 in 2004.

of people who attended Super Bowl XLI in 2007. Television ratings top more than 100 million viewers worldwide.

Anywhere from 16 to 19 races make up the Formula One season. In each race, 22 drivers compete on specially designed racecourses or blocked-off city streets. Races are held all around the world. Drivers earn points in each race depending on how they finish, and the driver with the most points at the end of the season is the champion.

The Best of the Best

Every sport has its share of superstars, but there always seems to be one or two of them who shine brighter than all the rest. Basketball has Michael Jordan. Baseball has Babe Ruth. Hockey has Wayne Gretzky. And Formula One racing has Michael Schumacher as its super-superstar.

Schumacher won seven Formula One championships in his career—the most of any driver in history. Five of those were won while racing for the Ferrari team.

When Schumacher joined the team in 1996, Ferrari had not won a championship since 1979. In just a few years, the German driver turned the team around. With Schumacher at the wheel, Ferrari won five straight titles, from 2000 to 2004.

Until his retirement following the 2006 season, Schumacher was one of the world's most famous athletes. His outstanding success on the track, including records for most race wins and most season championships, helped him earn more than $80 million a year.

Drivers race for teams, which are often owned by car companies such as Ferrari, Renault, and BMW. These sponsors pay for the car as well as salaries for the driver and crew members. The sponsors' names are painted on the car. The more money they pay, the bigger their name appears on the car. Sponsors want fans to know their names so they will buy their products. After all, running a Formula One team is not cheap—it can cost from $50 million to $200 million a year.

From Grand Prix to Formula One

Formula One was once officially known as Grand Prix racing. *Grand Prix* is a French term for "large prize." The first Grand Prix race was held in Le Mans, France, in 1906. The first Formula One Championship was run in 1950.

Three cars go into a tight turn during the 2005 Grand Prix of Long Beach race in California.

In the 1950s, Formula One cars were like regular passenger cars, with the engine in front. Big changes in car design came in the 1960s and 1970s. By 1961, all Formula One car engines were placed behind the driver. Airfoils, or wings, appeared on the cars in the 1970s and gave them more stability.

Indy

Open-wheel racing came to the United States in 1909. The biggest and most popular of these races was the Indianapolis 500 (called the "Indy 500" for short), held in Indiana. The first Indy 500 was held in 1911. The style of cars on the circuit became known as Indy cars, after the famous race.

Formula One driver Kimi Raikkonen of Finland drives for the Ferrari team. He is pictured during a race in Spain in 2007.

A driver (right) sits in his race car next to his mechanic at Indianapolis Motor Speedway in 1936.

Indy cars were similar to passenger cars in the early 1900s. Cars had two seats, one for the driver and one for a mechanic. The design of the cars began to change in the 1960s to look more like today's Formula One cars.

Safety features also improved after three drivers and a crew member died as a result of crashes at the Indy 500 in 1972 and 1973. Since then, safety features have constantly been updated to help keep drivers, crew members, and spectators from harm.

In past decades, there were several racing series that included Indy cars. But today, there are just two Indy-type series of races in the United States: Champ Series and IndyCar.

Like Formula One, IndyCar and Champ Series drivers race for teams owned by companies or sponsors.

Champ Series

From 1979 to 2004, the Championship Auto Racing Teams (CART) series was a popular series of Indy-type races. But eventually, many of the teams left it to go to the Indy Racing League (IRL).

The final Champ Car World Series race of the season is held in Mexico City. Sebastien Bourdais of France (above) won the race in 2006 and became that year's season champion.

The Most Famous Race in the World

The Indianapolis Motor Speedway opened in August 1909. The first race drew a crowd of 80,000. The speedway was later enlarged. It is now the biggest sports arena in the world—it can hold more than 400,000 fans! The Indianapolis 500 is the speedway's most famous race.

Up to 33 cars are allowed in the race. Drivers race 200 laps around the 2.5-mile track for a total of 500 miles, which is how the race got its name. Today, drivers top speeds of 220 mph.

At one time, the track was paved with bricks. In 1936, asphalt replaced the bricks, but the nickname "the brickyard" survived.

After the Indy 500, the winner drinks milk. The tradition started in 1936 when winner Louis Meyer drank some milk. A dairy executive saw a photo of this and decided that milk should be a part of every Indy 500 victory celebration.

Rick Mears celebrates his Indy 500 victory in 1991.

When the CART series went bankrupt in 2004, some remaining team owners decided to buy it. They renamed it the Champ Car World Series. The Champ Series season runs from March to November. It held 18 events in 2006.

Indy Racing League

The IRL was formed in 1996. Its first season had only four races with many unknown drivers. Today's IRL, however, features some of the best-known drivers from the United States and other countries.

The IRL season now has 14 races and runs from March to September. The most famous race on the circuit is the Indy 500. The IRL circuit is also known as IndyCar.

A Changing Sport

The sport of open-wheel racing has gone through many changes, and is still changing all the time. For example, in 2005, Danica Patrick, a 23-year-old woman driver, finished fourth in the Indy 500. It was the best performance by a woman in Indy history, and it drew many new fans to the sport of open-wheel racing.

CHAPTER 2

The Cars

Formula One, Indy, and Champ cars are nothing like your family's set of wheels. They are specially built to handle the curves and straight sections, or straightaways, of a racetrack at high speeds.

Chassis

An open-wheel car's chassis (CHASS-ee) is made from a strong material called carbon fiber. It forms the main structure— or "skeleton"—of the car. The wheels and engine are attached to the chassis. The chassis must be tough enough to protect the driver in a crash, but light enough to keep from weighing down the car.

Tires

A regular car tire can last 10,000 miles or more. But a typical open-wheel race car tire will last for only about 120 miles—at the

IndyCar and Champ Series cars use slicks, which are tires with no grooves (left). Formula One cars use grooved tires (right).

most. This is because of the extreme pressure, heat, and wear-and-tear of racing at high speeds. Open-wheel race car tires are about twice the size of tires on regular cars, and are made of soft rubber to grip the track.

Formula One cars used non-treaded "slick" tires until a 1998 rule change. They now ride on grooved tires to keep speeds down on the corners. This makes racing safer.

IndyCar and Champ Series cars still use "slicks." When the car is racing along the track, the tire surface gets so hot that it becomes sticky. This helps the tire grip the ground. However, grooved tires are used in wet weather for safety. They will not slip as much as slicks on a wet track.

Engine

Formula One cars use small, powerful engines that produce 830 horsepower (hp). That is about three times as powerful as a regular passenger car. Champ Series cars and IndyCars use slightly less powerful engines, with 750 hp (Champ Series) and 650 hp (IndyCar).

WILD FACT

Horsepower is a measure of engine performance. It compares the power created by one horse to what an engine can do. This means it would take 830 horses working together to produce enough power to drive a Formula One car at top speed!

fuel injection

cylinder head

engine block

end of the crank shaft

A Formula One race car engine

The intense heat and energy put out by any race car engine almost tears it apart. Rubber parts melt, plastic parts break, and metal parts are heated up enough to weaken them. In the past, each engine used to be rebuilt almost from scratch with new parts after every race because of this. But in 2006, all cars in the IRL began using a new engine designed to better withstand the harsh conditions of racing. After each race, these engines are taken apart and the parts are

WILD

FACT

The cockpit of an open-wheel racer is a tight squeeze. A driver has to remove the steering wheel to get into and out of the car!

carefully examined to make sure they are still in top shape. Then the engines are rebuilt for the next race, using whatever new parts are necessary.

Body

While the chassis of an open-wheel racer is like the car's skeleton, the outer shell, or body, is like the car's skin. It is made of lightweight carbon fiber or other high-tech plastic, and fiberglass. The body is also designed to cut cleanly through the air at top speeds. It can be put on and taken off the chassis easily in case it is damaged in a race.

The car's body must be a certain length and height according to the rules of each circuit. This ensures that all of the cars are equal in

A camera attached to a Formula One race car gives television viewers a driver's-eye look at the race.

design and one does not have an advantage over another.

The inside area of the body that holds the driver's cockpit is called the "tub." The body's outside is painted a bright color and covered with the names of the team sponsors.

All Formula One cars have up to five cameras attached to them during every race. The cameras are used during live television coverage of the races to give fans a racer's-eye view of the action.

Wings

Airplanes have wings to help get them off the ground. Open-wheel cars have "wings," too, but these wings are attached to the front and rear of the car.

camera

rear wing

roll bar

front wing

Open-wheel race cars have wings, also called airfoils, at the front and rear.

A Safe Cocoon

Inside an open-wheel racer is the cockpit—the driver's "survival cell." Many drivers have walked away from crashes because of the safety features of the survival cell. For example, padded, upside-down U-shaped roll bars in front of and behind the driver shield the driver if the car overturns. The weight of the car will fall on the roll bars and not the driver.

Padding in the cockpit and a helmet protect the driver's head in case of a crash. But the driver must also wear the Head and Neck Support (HANS) device. It is a collar that attaches to the driver's helmet. The HANS device keeps the driver's head and neck from moving around during a race. This reduces the risk of injury.

HANS device

Also, the cars' wings do the opposite of airplane wings. Instead of helping to lift the car off the ground, they press the car harder onto the track. This is called "downforce." It gives the car more traction, or ability to stick to the track. This helps the car to speed up, brake, and turn corners.

Formula One, Indy, Champ: *A Closer Look*

Formula One

Indy Racing League

Champ Series

	Formula One	Indy Racing League	Champ Series
TOP SPEED	230 mph	230 mph	240 mph
HORSEPOWER	830 hp	650 hp	750 hp
TIRES	Grooved	Ungrooved	Ungrooved
WHEELBASE (distance between front and rear wheels)	120–130 inches	110 inches (minimum)	124–128 inches
WEIGHT	1,322 pounds with driver	1,550 pounds without driver	1,565 pounds without driver
HEIGHT	37.43 inches	38 inches	32 inches
WIDTH	70.87 inches	78.5 inches	78.5 inches

A Formula One car without wheels sits in its garage area, ready to be worked on. This was before a race at Laguna Seca in California in 2006.

CHAPTER 3

At the Track

The goal of any race car driver is to win—plain and simple. Every member of the team works extremely hard at every race to reach that goal.

A lot of hard work goes into getting a team's equipment ready for a race weekend. Races are held all over the world, so teams are always on the go. Formula One, IndyCar, and Champ Series teams carry extra cars, spare parts, tires, tools, and computers in huge 18-wheel trucks. Teams arrive at the track on Wednesday or Thursday to set up portable garages for the weekend ahead.

All events start with practice sessions. These sessions are important for all race car drivers and teams. They give the drivers a feel for the track before the race. It is also the last time the mechanics can work on the cars' brakes, engine, and anything else that may need adjusting.

Drivers and team managers attend a pre-race meeting at every event. Here, the race director goes over the rules and regulations.

A day or two before each race, the drivers must qualify for starting positions. To qualify, the drivers race around the track. The ones

WILD FACT

Every driver must attend the pre-race meeting. In fact, if a driver misses the meeting, he or she is fined and can be thrown out of the race!

Sam Hornish, Jr., earned the pole position in the 2006 Indy 500. As the race starts, his car is the one in front on the right, closest to the inside of the track.

with the fastest times get to participate in the race. Their times also determine where the cars line up on the starting grid. (The starting grid is the position the cars take at the start of the race.)

The driver with the best time gets the best spot—the pole position. This is the inside lane of the first row. The driver in the pole position starts the race in the lead and has the shortest and fastest route around the track for the first lap of the race. The other cars line up two-by-two in rows behind, positioned eight meters (about 26 feet) apart.

Types of Tracks

Formula One races are about 180 miles long and last two hours. They are held on different types of courses around the world. Most are on racetracks with straightaways and curves to test the drivers' skills. Some, such as the Monaco Grand Prix in Europe, take place on narrow, curvy city streets that have been closed to traffic. IndyCar and Champ Series races cover distances of 150 to 500 miles and last from two to four hours.

The Grand Prix of Monaco is run on a road course that is just over two miles long. It is one of the most difficult courses in Formula One.

There are three types of tracks—ovals, superovals, and road courses. Ovals, or speedways, measure between 0.75 and 2.5 miles. The Indy 500 is run on this type of track. Superovals, or superspeedways, are at least 1.5 miles and have steeply banked (slanted) turns.

The Milwaukee Mile in Wisconsin is an example of an oval, or speedway. It is an IndyCar race course.

Road courses are between 1.5 and 4 miles. They can be on a permanent track or on a special track set up on city streets. The Streets of Long Beach race in California is run on city streets that are usually very busy—when they are not cleared for the race!

Flags

Colorful flags quickly tell drivers what is going on during a race. Drivers have to look out for the flags, like regular drivers must be on the lookout for traffic signals and road signs.

START racing!

Take CAUTION—there may be an accident on the track. All drivers must slow down to a lower speed and cannot pass other cars until the track is cleared.

STOP! It could be bad weather or a bad accident, and the race has been stopped. All drivers must leave the track.

Busted! A driver has gotten a PENALTY for unsafe driving and must leave the track, either for one lap or the rest of the race.

Slower cars must MOVE OVER for faster cars (in Formula One, the flag is plain blue).

Be careful—there is OIL ON THE TRACK. Oil makes the track slick, so drive carefully through this area.

There is an EMERGENCY VEHICLE on the track (Champ Series; IndyCar is a red cross, while Formula One is plain white).

It is the LAST LAP (IndyCar/Champ Series); there is an emergency or a slow-moving vehicle on the track (Formula One).

It is the END OF THE RACE. The first driver to pass this flag is the winner!

CHAPTER 4

Race and Strategy

Speeding along at 200 mph, the driver is strapped tightly into the cockpit. The engine roars. The car is vibrating. The inside of the cockpit is like an oven because of the engine's heat. (Cockpit temperatures can reach 120 degrees on hot days!) It is tough to concentrate under these conditions. But a race car driver must stay focused. Formula One and Champ Series races last for two hours. Most IndyCar races last for two and a half hours. The Indy 500 lasts even longer— three to four hours.

Drivers must remain aware of their competitors and what they are doing. They have to look out for flags to see what is happening in the race. At the same time, they use their cockpit radios to talk with their crews to tell them how the car is running. Likewise, the crews tell them when to push harder or take it easy.

Drivers have to handle the challenges of different tracks. Racing on longer tracks with a lot of straightaways means more passing. On curved tracks, there is more cornering and braking. Road courses have such tight turns that drivers cannot afford to make any mistakes.

Working Together to Win

Besides getting into a good position, a driver must make sure that the car has enough fuel and that the tires have enough grip for the entire race. When it is time to refuel or change tires that have worn out due to the hard racing, the pit crew calls the driver into the pit area. Each team has its own pit area. Drivers can make several pit stops during a race.

A successful pit stop can often be the difference in winning or losing a race. Every

In the Pits

As many as 18 or 20 people might work on a car during a pit stop. These are the basic jobs:

Jack man: Connects an air hose at the rear of the car's chassis to lift it for a tire change.

Rear tire changer (far side): After the tire is changed, this crew member helps push the car out of the pit area.

Rear tire changer (near side): Helps push the car out of the pit area after the tire is changed.

team's pit crew is ready for action. Each member has a job to do. A pit crew practices its jobs just as any athlete works on his or her game. A good pit crew can change all four tires and refuel a car in less than ten seconds! The pit crew can be just as important as the driver in winning a race. Together, they work hard to make their team number one.

Oil spills, debris on the track, and accidents can happen during a race. When one of these things occurs, the yellow flag is waved. Drivers know to slow down until the track is clear.

Front tire changer (far side): Guides the driver into the team's pit area. After changing the tire, this crew member adjusts the wings and lets the driver know when to leave the pit.

Lollipop man: Holds a stop sign ("lollipop") so the driver knows where to stop.

Front tire changer (near side): This crew member can change a tire in six to eight seconds since there is no need to run around the car.

Fuel man: Refuels the car by putting the nozzle into the opening of the fuel tank.

The race is over when the first car crosses the finish line after all the laps have been run. As the checkered flag drops, the winning team high-fives each other and starts celebrating. The fans shout for their favorites. After a victory lap around the track, the top-finishing cars roll into Victory Lane. Reporters and photographers crowd around to capture the moment. After the drivers climb from their cars and wave to the fans, the winning driver and sometimes the top two finishers receive their trophies in Victory Lane. After an Indy 500 win, it is a tradition for drivers to drink milk. Formula One and Champ Series drivers often spray champagne on their teammates and the reporters.

It has been a hard few hours of driving, and the driver is tired and hot. But he does not feel tired at all if he is standing on that podium holding up a gleaming trophy . . . and getting a big cash prize!

Jenson Button of Great Britain sends out a shower of champagne after a good finish in the 2004 Formula One Grand Prix of Europe.

Real Athletes

Car racing requires a lot of endurance. This means that drivers need a lot of strength for a long period of time. Some people argue that race car drivers are not real athletes. But drivers must have strength, stamina, quick reflexes, good vision, and great concentration to perform at their best. Drivers train as hard as other athletes. They run, swim, and bike to stay in shape. They do exercises

Getting Technical

Race car drivers just drive around in circles, right? Wrong. It takes loads of skill to handle a race car. These are just two of the techniques drivers use on the track:

Drafting: When a car is traveling at 200 mph, it creates a wind tunnel. This reduces the wind resistance for the car directly behind it. That car actually gets sucked along by the wind. A good driver can use this "draft" to pass the car in front or let up on the gas a bit to save fuel.

Cornering: While driving on the straightaways of a racetrack is all about power, turning corners takes a lot of skill. The driver must brake, turn, and then accelerate (speed up) out of the turn. Cornering can be dangerous, and takes practice.

to build strong arms, necks, and chests. Drivers also watch what they eat. They eat energy-boosting foods and drink lots of water before a race to make sure they have enough stamina. They must stay calm, alert, and level-headed. They must rely on their quick thinking to make it to the finish line.

CHAPTER 5

The Best Drivers

Most race car drivers start racing go-karts when they are kids. If they are really good, they can eventually compete at the national level, against young people from all over the country. Then they may move on to international competition. From go-karts, drivers can then progress to other types of racing, such as Formula Three (in Europe), Sprint Car Series, Midget Car Series, and Formula 2000 (in the United States). Then, drivers hope to move up to the "major leagues" of racing: IRL, Champ, or Formula One. They work their way up to the highest level by impressing team owners with their skills and experience. They hope the team owners will hire them to race for their team.

Many people consider open-wheel drivers to be the most talented drivers in the world. They have incredible skill and daring on the track. Here are some of the best racers today:

Fernando Alonso, Spain: In 2005, Alonso did something that seemed impossible. He took the Formula One championship away from Michael Schumacher. It was the first time in five years a driver other than

Schumacher had won the crown. At age 24, Alonso became the youngest champion in Formula One history. More amazing, he did it in his third season of Formula One racing. Alonso went on to win the championship again in 2006.

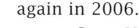

Sam Hornish, Jr., United States: At age 21, Hornish was the youngest driver to win an IndyCar race. He is a three-time IRL champion (2001, 2002, and 2006), and the only driver to win back-to-back championships. Hornish won the 2006 Indy 500 with an exciting finish. He passed rookie Marco Andretti at the end of the race and beat him by 0.0635

Sam Hornish, Jr., poses after his exciting 2006 Indy 500 win.

of a second. It was the second-closest finish in Indy history.

Tony Kanaan, Brazil: Kanaan won the 2004 IRL Championship. He had 15-straight top-five finishes, including three wins and six second-place finishes. Kanaan completed all 3,305 laps of the races he was in—the first IndyCar driver to do so.

A Driver's Gear

Drivers are covered from head to toe with gear for protection in case of fire.

Helmet: A padded helmet covers the driver's face completely. It is made of carbon fiber material, similar to a race car's chassis and body.

Driving suit: A driver must wear a one-piece fire-resistant suit. Even the underwear is fire-resistant!

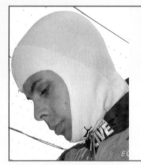

Balaclava: This fire-resistant hood is worn under the helmet. It is more protection for the driver's head.

Shoes: Shoes are made of leather or suede. They are lined with fire-resistant material and have rubber soles for grip.

Gloves: Fire-resistant gloves have leather palms for gripping the steering wheel.

Sebastien Bourdais, France: Bourdais (bor-DAY) won the Champ Car World Series title three times (2004, 2005, and 2006) in just five seasons on the circuit. Before joining the Champ Car Series, Bourdais tore up the Formula 3000 (F3000) circuit, the training ground for Formula One.

Paul Tracy, Canada: Tracy was the 2003 Champ Car World Series champion. He also rules the track at the Grand Prix of Long Beach, which he has won four times. Tracy is in the top seven all-time in wins (30), pole positions (25), and laps led (4,184).

What About Women Racers?

Many women have played a part as drivers in open-wheel racing. A few have made their mark at the Indy 500.

Janet Guthrie: In 1977, Guthrie was the first woman to start in the Indy 500. She raced two more times (1978 and 1979). Guthrie's best finish was ninth place in 1978. When she qualified for Indy in 1978, Guthrie broke her own women's world record. She raised the record to 191.002 mph.

Lyn St. James: St. James competed in the Indy 500 seven times (1992–1997, 2000), the most of any woman. St. James finished 11th in 1992 and was named the Indy 500 Rookie of the Year. She set the women's world record in closed-course speed in 1995, reaching 225.722 mph. St. James earned more than $1 million participating in the Indy 500.

Sarah Fisher: Fisher started her first Indy 500 race in 2000 at age 19. She was the youngest woman and third-youngest driver ever to compete in the race. Fisher participated in the race for the next four years. Her best finish was 21st place in 2004. Fisher's Indy 500 earnings total more than $1 million.

Danica Patrick: The IRL got a boost in popularity with Patrick's success. She was named IRL Rookie of the Year in 2005 after finishing

Danica Patrick relaxes before the 2006 Indy 500. She came in eighth in the race.

We Are Family

Children often grow up and join the family business. Kids born into racing families are no different. Here are just a few who have joined their relatives in racing.

Driver	Relationship	Years Competing
Mario Andretti		1964–1994
Jeff Andretti	son of Mario	1990–2000
Michael Andretti	son of Mario	1983–present
Marco Andretti	son of Michael	2006–present
John Andretti	nephew of Mario	1987–present
A.J. Foyt		1957–1993
Larry Foyt	son of A.J.	2003–present
A.J. Foyt IV	grandson of A.J.	2003–present
Rick Mears		1978–1992
Roger Mears	brother of Rick	1978–1984
Casey Mears	son of Roger	2001–present
Jerry Unser		1958–1959
Bobby Unser	brother of Jerry	1962–1982
Al Unser	brother of Jerry	1964–1994
Al Unser, Jr.	son of Al	1982–2004
Johnny Unser	son of Jerry	1993–2000
Robby Unser	son of Bobby	1998–2000

fourth in the Indy 500. It was the best finish for a woman in the history of the race. Patrick led the race for 19 laps, becoming the only woman to lead the Indy field. She finished eighth in 2006. In just two years racing at Indy, Patrick earned $664,600.

All-time Best

Michael Schumacher, Germany: Schumacher was the best in Formula One racing from the mid-1990s to his retirement in 2006. He won the driver's championship a record seven times (1994, 1995, and 2000–2004).

Mario Andretti, United States: Andretti is often called the greatest race car driver in history. He is certainly the best all-around driver. Andretti is the only driver to win the Daytona 500, a NASCAR race (1967), the Indy 500 (1969), and the Formula One championship (1978). He is also a four-time IndyCar champion (1965, 1966, 1969, and 1984). In 1993, Andretti became the oldest winner in IndyCar history at 53 years and 34 days. He retired in 1994.

A.J. Foyt, United States: Foyt is the only driver to win the Indy 500, the 24 Hours of Le Mans, and the Daytona 500. He is the first

A.J. Foyt prepares for the 1962 Indy 500. Although he did not win the race that year, he had won it the year before and would win it three more times in his career.

driver to win the Indy 500 four times (1961, 1964, 1967, and 1977). Foyt won the season championship seven times and is the all-time leader in victories with 67. He started a record 35 straight Indy 500s from 1958 to 1992. Foyt retired in 1993.

Rick Mears, United States: Mears won the Indy 500 four times (1979, 1984, 1988, and 1991). He became the youngest driver (at 39) to have four victories. Mears also won three CART championships (1979, 1981, and 1982). He retired from racing in 1992.

Today, a future group of world-class drivers is busy perfecting its skills in the "minor leagues" of open-wheel racing. Those drivers will work their way up until they are good enough to compete against the best in the world.

airfoils—Wings that are attached to the front and rear of a race car for stability.

asphalt—Tar-like substance mixed with sand and gravel that is used to pave racetracks.

balaclava—A fire-resistant hood that drivers wear under their helmets.

carbon fiber—A strong but lightweight material used to make the chassis and body of a race car.

chassis—The skeleton or frame of a car.

cockpit—The area of the chassis where the driver sits.

downforce—The pressure created when air pushes a car's tires to the ground.

grid—The starting order of cars in a race, determined by qualifying times.

grip—A car's ability to stay in contact with the racetrack when accelerating, braking, and turning a corner.

HANS device—Short for Head and Neck Support. A safety collar worn by drivers to keep the head and neck stable during a race, reducing the risk of head and neck injuries.

horsepower (hp)—A measure of engine performance and power. It compares the power created by one horse to what an engine can do. For example, it would take 830 horses working together to create the same power as a 830-hp Formula One engine.

pit crew—Members of a driver's team who refuel the car and change its tires during a race.

pole position—The spot where the driver with the fastest qualifying time starts the race. It is the inside of the front row, which is the shortest distance around the track.

slicks—Ungrooved racing tires used by Champ Series and Indy Racing League cars.

straightaways—The straight sections of a racetrack.

Victory Lane—Part of the track reserved for the race winner and the top finishers to park their cars and stand on a platform to receive their trophies.

Further Reading

Books

Arron, Simon, and Mark Hughes. *The Complete Book of Formula One.* Minneapolis: Motorbooks, 2003.

Fish, Bruce, and Becky Durost Fish. *Indy Car Racing.* New York: Chelsea House, 2001.

Hilton, Christopher. *Michael Schumacher: The Greatest of All.* Yeovil, Somerset, U.K.: Haynes Publishing, 2004.

Indy-Tech Publishing. *Danica Patrick.* Indianapolis: Sams Technical Publishing, 2005.

Internet Addresses

http://www.champcarworldseries.com The official Web site of the Champ Car World Series, with information on schedules and drivers.

http://www.formula1.com Formula One's official Web site includes a Hall of Fame.

http://www.indycar.com IndyCar fans can participate in lots of online activities on this official Web site.

Index